THE MUSIC INSIDE US

*To Evelyn Wadkins, my fabulous cello teacher; her wife, Melanie Wadkins; and their children, Cece and Miguel—all very dear friends who bring out the music inside me*

—J.H.

*To Jim & Wendi, two musician-agains*

—J.W.

The illustrations in this book were made with acrylic, crayon, watercolor, and digital editing.

The illustrator acknowledges the support of Arts Nova Scotia.

Cataloging-in-Publication Data has been applied for and may be obtained from the Library of Congress.

ISBN 978-1-4197-5521-7
eISBN 978-1-64700-343-2

Text © 2025 James Howe
Illustrations © 2025 Jack Wong
Book design by Melissa Nelson Greenberg

Published in 2025 by Abrams Books for Young Readers, an imprint of ABRAMS. All rights reserved. No portion of this book may be reproduced, stored in a retrieval system, or transmitted in any form or by any means, mechanical, electronic, photocopying, recording, or otherwise, without written permission from the publisher.

Printed and bound in China
10 9 8 7 6 5 4 3 2 1

Abrams Books for Young Readers are available at special discounts when purchased in quantity for premiums and promotions as well as fundraising or educational use. Special editions can also be created to specification. For details, contact specialsales@abramsbooks.com or the address below.

ABRAMS  The Art of Books
195 Broadway, New York, NY 10007
abramsbooks.com

# THE MUSIC INSIDE US

## YO-YO MA & His Gifts to the World

written by James Howe
illustrated by Jack Wong

ABRAMS BOOKS FOR YOUNG READERS • NEW YORK

"I've been asking myself all my life,
'What is the purpose of music?'"

In a small apartment in Paris
lived a boy named Yo-Yo Ma.

Everyone made music in this small apartment.
His mother sang.
His sister played the piano and the violin.
His father played the violin
and taught both his children to play.

But Yo-Yo did not want
to play the violin.
He wanted to play a BIG instrument.

So he learned to play the cello,
although the cello he played was a small one, as cellos go,
because Yo-Yo was only four years old.

Everyone is born with gifts inside them.
Yo-Yo was no exception,
though his gifts were exceptional.

Music flowed through him with an
understanding and mastery beyond his years.
He had a bright and curious mind.
Learning came quickly and easily.

At first, Yo-Yo was taught by his father.
But as his father did not play the cello himself,
he found Yo-Yo one of the best cello teachers in Paris:
Madame Michelle Lepinte.

Yo-Yo loved Madame Lepinte.
She was kind and encouraging.
And she was amazed by her new student.
To think that a four-year-old could play
an entire Bach cello suite from memory!

Yo-Yo and his sister, Yeou-Cheng, spent hours practicing their instruments, mastering one short passage of music each day.

In their father's room—the room Yo-Yo called "the room of too much work"—Yo-Yo and Yeou-Cheng were taught ear training, harmony, and music theory. Their father also taught them to speak and write in Chinese and French, since they were Chinese by birth and lived in France.

Their lessons and practice took up much of their day.
They had little time for friends or play.

Because he was so smart and quick to learn,
Yo-Yo often grew bored and restless
practicing and studying.

He was full of energy and loved to be silly.
He hopped around his small apartment like a frog.
He played tricks on his sister,
some of which made her laugh.

Making his sister laugh made Yo-Yo happy.
Making music with his sister made him happy, too.
He on his cello, she on her violin or piano,
two instruments blending,
two musicians listening intently to each other.

Two children learning to make music as one.

It wasn't long before Yo-Yo and his sister were performing for other people.

The people who heard them were amazed by how well they played.
Yo-Yo only five years old, Yeou-Cheng only nine.

When Yo-Yo was seven, a big change happened in his life.

He and his family moved to America. They chose to live in New York City, where Yo-Yo could study with some of the greatest teachers in the world.

Life in America was confusing for Yo-Yo, but it was exciting, too.

Everything was different from what he was used to—
the language, the people, the way things were done.

The differences made his world bigger,
and that was what was exciting about it!

It wasn't long after he arrived in America that he met and played for the legendary cellist Pablo Casals. Thanks to Casals, Yo-Yo was invited to play on television before the President of the United States!

Yeou-Cheng accompanied him on the piano.

Many people across the country saw their performance and were astounded by these shy yet confident children who played with such command.

He began studying with acclaimed cellist and cello teacher Leonard Rose. He became the principal cellist in his father's children's orchestra. He would soon play at Carnegie Hall.

His mind was filling up with questions about the bigger world and his place in it.

Yo-Yo did not have words for all these questions yet.
He was still a child and had been taught by his parents
to be obedient and not ask too many questions.

So he kept his questions in his head and played the cello
because that was what he was expected to do
and what he was good at doing.

One day he had a question for his mother about the sonata he was struggling to play.

"Will you sing it for me?" he asked.

When she had finished, he wanted to know
how she could make it so full of feeling when he couldn't.

After a moment's thought, she told her son that even without training,
a singer can express their deepest feelings through their voice.
A cellist, like all musicians who play instruments, must work for a long time,
developing their technique until their instrument becomes their voice.
Then the instrument will be able to pour out the feelings a singer expresses naturally.

His question to his mother that day gave him the answer he needed
to grow his gift for music into something deeper, something bigger.

For years, Yo-Yo worked hard on his technique,
listening carefully as he played,
until his cello sang with its own voice,
in harmony with *his* voice,

his heart.

his body.

his soul.

By the time he had turned twelve, he had become well-known
and was being compared to the greatest cellists of the century.

Invitations poured in for him to perform,
many of which his father turned down,
as he had done from the time Yo-Yo was little
and just beginning to perform in Paris.

It was important, his father said, that he continue
to grow as a musician before becoming the shining star
he was certain Yo-Yo was destined to be.

As a teenager, Yo-Yo had his own reasons to take time away from performing.

He had more questions that needed answers, and they were not answers his father or his mother or even his music could give him.

When he was fifteen, Yo-Yo began spending his summers at music camp.
Away from his home and family,
he was free to be himself in ways he had never been before,
to think for himself, act for himself,
explore the *more* of this person named Yo-Yo Ma.

After visiting his older sister in college,
Yo-Yo made a bold decision.
He would continue to perform—he was much in demand!—
but he would also go to college for four years.

There, he hoped to find out if he could do anything else but play the cello.
He wanted to learn more about the world and understand his place in it.

In college, his favorite course was anthropology, the study of human societies and cultures. Yo-Yo was curious about what makes groups of people different from one another and also what connects them.

He found something that every group of people in the world has in common—

## music!

The instruments they play or the sounds their mouths make may be different, but everywhere in the world, people are making music.
And each culture makes music that is uniquely its own.

Yo-Yo decided that he would spend his life not only performing for others, but learning from others about their musical traditions
and finding ways to bring cultures together through the music they make.

He would travel the world and ask questions of the people he met.

What does your music mean to you?

Where did it come from?

How do you play your instrument like that?

How do we connect by listening to each other, teaching each other, playing with each other?

In this way, he hoped he could bring people together in harmony and joy.

And so Yo-Yo Ma began the great adventure that would be his grown-up life.

He would perform and record music that was hundreds of years old,
like the very first piece he played for Madame Lepinte at the age of four.
He would play new music, some of it written just for him.
He would play alone, and he would play with others.
He would learn the music of Brazil and Argentina,
of Japan and the Appalachian Mountains.

He would ask, "What happens when strangers meet?"
And he would bring together musicians from all over the world
to learn from one another,
play with one another, create new music together,
turning strangers into friends.

He would play

on television for children,

with Elmo and Mister Rogers

and Arthur the Aardvark.

He would teach young cellists,

helping them master their technique

so that they could play in harmony with

*their* voices, their hearts and bodies and souls.

He would use his cello and his voice
to speak out against injustice and war.
He would play in protest.
He would play in celebration.

He would play and speak out to
help bring harmony to a troubled
and divided world.

When he could not travel and perform during
the time of the COVID pandemic,
he would perform online, alone, at home,
making videos to offer music
and comfort and companionship to others
who were isolated and alone.

Yo-Yo Ma would become one of the greatest cellists of all time.

He would be honored by American presidents and organizations around the world for his efforts as a humanitarian working for world peace.

He would always be guided by the words Pablo Casals said to him when he was a child:

"I am a human being first, a musician second, a cellist third."

Not everyone is a cellist or a musician or an artist of any kind.
But everyone *is* a human being.

We are all born with gifts inside us,
our own music inside us.

And we can all ask the same kinds of questions
Yo-Yo Ma has never stopped asking.

Who am I?
Who are we?

How can we use the gifts inside us
to bring people harmony and joy
and make the world a better place
because we have been here?

"It's up to us to choose what
the future looks like."
—Yo-Yo Ma

# MORE ABOUT YO-YO MA

## 1955
Yo-Yo Ma is born on October 7 in Paris, France, given the Christian name "Ernest" and the Chinese name "Yo," which means "friend." Thinking that "Yo Ma" doesn't sound very musical, his parents add a second "Yo," giving their son a name as musical and unique as the child himself.

## 1958–1959
At three, Yo-Yo begins studying piano and violin with his father. At four, he takes up the cello.

## 1962
Yo-Yo moves to New York City. He plays in Washington, D.C., before President John F. Kennedy and former president Dwight D. Eisenhower, among other dignitaries. The New York Philharmonic conductor and composer Leonard Bernstein welcomes Yo-Yo and his family as immigrants, introducing Yo-Yo as "a seven-year-old Chinese cellist playing old French music for his new American compatriots."

## 1964
Yo-Yo is admitted to the Pre-College division of Juilliard School while also attending the École Française. He makes his first appearance as a cello soloist with an orchestra.

## 1968
He leaves the École Française and enters the Professional Children's School, a school for working child actors and musicians.

## 1971
Yo-Yo graduates from the Professional Children's School at age fifteen, makes his professional debut at the Weill Recital Hall at Carnegie Hall, and meets pianist Emanuel Ax, who becomes his lifelong friend and musical collaborator. He spends the summer at Meadowmount School of Music, getting his first taste of independence.

## 1972
Yo-Yo spends the summer at Marlboro Music Festival in Vermont, where he meets Jill Hornor, who will later become his wife. He enters Harvard University.

## 1976
Yo-Yo graduates from Harvard with a BA in anthropology and humanities.

## 1978
He marries Jill Hornor; wins the Avery Fisher Prize, the first of many notable prizes and honors he will receive; and makes his debut with the New York Philharmonic Orchestra.

## 1980
Yo-Yo undergoes surgery to correct scoliosis, a curvature of the spine, risking nerve damage and his ability to play the cello professionally. The operation is a success. He even gains two inches in height!

## 1983
His first child, Nicholas, is born.

## 1984
Yo-Yo becomes the first Chinese American to win a Grammy Award for recording. (He will go on to win many more.)

## 1985
His daughter, Emily, is born. He makes his first appearance on *Mister Rogers' Neighborhood*.

## 1987
In the first of several appearances on *Sesame Street*, Yo-Yo jams with the Honkers and helps Elmo learn to the play the violin.

## 1992
He records the bestselling album *Hush* with folk-jazz vocalist Bobby McFerrin, who encourages him to improvise, something that does not come easily to the classically trained cellist. When they perform together for the first time, Yo-Yo has a bad case of nerves. He says, "I'm not brave. I'm actually pretty scared most of the time. But I must like being scared because I keep doing things that scare me."

## 1993
Yo-Yo visits the San people in the Kalahari Desert in Africa to learn about their music and traditions. He makes a documentary about the trip called *Distant Echoes*, which is released in 1997.

## 1998
He founds the Silk Road Project (now called Silkroad), a collective of artists from around the world who create, perform, and record music from their various traditions. In the same year, *Yo-Yo Ma Inspired by Bach* (broadcast in 1997) received numerous awards. Aired on PBS, the series of six short films is based on the Bach Cello Suites, and Yo-Yo creates the films in collaboration with artists from other disciplines, including a choreographer, an architect, and a pair of world champion ice dancers!

## 1999
With garden designer Julie Moir Messervy, Yo-Yo creates the Toronto Music Garden, inspired by the first Bach Cello Suite. He also guest stars as a cartoon version of himself on the popular series *Arthur*. In October, exhausted after playing at Carnegie Hall, he forgets his eighteenth-century cello, valued at $2.5 million, in the trunk of a NYC taxicab. The cello, nicknamed Petunia, turns up—unharmed—four days later at the cab company.

## 2001
Yo-Yo is presented with the National Medal of Arts.

## 2006
Yo-Yo is designated a Messenger of Peace by the United Nations.

## 2009
He plays at the inaugural ceremony of President Barack Obama.

## 2011
He is presented with the Presidential Medal of Freedom.

## 2013
He is awarded the Vilcek Foundation Prize honoring the musical achievements of immigrant artists in the United States.

## 2014
Yo-Yo is the first recipient of the Fred Rogers Legacy Award. Because of their shared values and deep respect for children, he and Fred Rogers become lifelong friends. Accepting the award, Yo-Yo says, "This is perhaps the greatest honor I've ever received."

## 2018
Yo-Yo launches the Bach Project, setting out to perform the six cello suites in one sitting in thirty-six locations around the world. Each concert is followed by a day of community building through conversations, collaborations, and performances.

## 2020
He streams a performance series, "Songs of Comfort and Hope," on YouTube and social media to reach out to people quarantined during the COVID pandemic.

## 2021
On January 26, Yo-Yo plays at the inaugural ceremony of President Joe Biden.

On March 14, in the fifteen minutes required to wait after being vaccinated for COVID-19, he takes out his cello and plays an impromptu concert for the others who are waiting. It is possible that some of those hearing him do not know who he is. But when he finishes, they break into applause as Yo-Yo waves, then packs up his cello to go home.

## AUTHOR'S NOTE

Like Yo-Yo Ma, I played the cello as a child, although unlike Yo-Yo Ma, I didn't take it up until the end of the sixth grade and gave it up less than a year later. I'm not sure why I didn't continue, though I suspect it had something to do with that resounding off-key final note I hit when my orchestra class performed in concert. When the teacher played the recorded concert at our next class, my off-key note came through loud and clear, and with it, my red-faced humiliation and the thought that the cello and I were perhaps not meant for each other.

I didn't think much about the cello until years later when, in my twenties, I went to see Yo-Yo Ma early in his career at Lincoln Center in New York City. I don't remember what he played, but I can still picture *how* he played. His head was lifted, his eyes were closed. He and his cello moved as one. I had never seen anyone play the way he did, with so much emotion and such obvious joy.

As more years passed, I had the good fortune of seeing Yo-Yo Ma play in person a number of other times. But I didn't think much about how he played until I decided I wanted to learn to play the cello again more than fifty years since I'd stopped. I found a wonderful teacher and plunged in, not giving a thought to how hard it might be to learn, and thankfully not remembering that ill-fated concert back in middle school.

When I was learning the first Bach Cello Suite—the very one Yo-Yo mastered when he was four!—I listened repeatedly and carefully to Yo-Yo's recording of it on his album *Six Evolutions*. I could hear in his playing what I heard in his other recordings and what I saw on the stage: how immersed he was in the music, how he and his cello were one. It made me want to go deeper in my playing. It also made me curious to know more about the man behind the music.

And so I wrote this book for the same reason that Yo-Yo Ma has done so much in his life: to ask questions and to learn, to let another's life touch and inspire my own, and to connect.

I worked on this book during the first years of the pandemic. During that time, Yo-Yo released several albums, including one with his friend and collaborator, the pianist Kathryn Stott. It was called *Songs of Comfort and Hope*, and it was meant to offer just that—comfort and hope to all of us going through a difficult and challenging time. I played the album often and was particularly taken with the piece "Rain Falling From the Roof," written by another long-time collaborator of Yo-Yo's, the composer Wu Tong. Listening carefully, and with the help of my teacher, I figured out the cello part and played along with the recording. What a joy it was to make music with Yo-Yo Ma as I wrote this story of his life!

JAMES HOWE

*Yo-Yo Ma, age nine*
Irving Penn/Conde Nast via Getty Images

# ILLUSTRATOR'S NOTE

When I was first contacted about illustrating a book James had written about Yo-Yo Ma, I admittedly didn't know very much about the cello. Through working on this book, I learned more about Yo-Yo and the cellists who influenced him, and about the music written for this magnificent instrument. I also learned a lot about other things, like bus designs in 1950s Paris, urban bird species in New York City, and the direction of the Milky Way Galaxy!

"The music inside us" that this book refers to is not necessarily a literal music that you play or listen to, but any passion or strength each of us may have that seems to flow like music, moving us from within, wanting to be heard. Along with being something beautiful in its own right, it's also a way for each of us to relate to the world. As an artist, drawing and painting are my ways of making sense of things that are new to me—just like Yo-Yo's music playing was his gateway to engaging in anthropology, travel, political action, and humanitarianism. So when I started to try to illustrate this story of Yo-Yo's life, I didn't have to feel daunted that his cello music was complex and sometimes beyond my understanding. Instead, I focused on the parts that I could understand through my own art—for example, a cello's shape, or its many subtle but dazzling colors, or how its end pin makes myriad marks on the floor over a lifetime of playing, just like a drawing tool (a phenomenon so interesting to me that I had to include it in this book—look under the dust jacket!).

In this sense, the music inside each of us is not only a gift to the world, but the gift to ourselves of always having a place to start whenever we face something new. I wonder what music inside of you stirred when you read this book—and where it'll take you!

JACK WONG

Yo-Yo Ma performs with DC Youth Orchestra

Photo by Paul Morigi/Getty Images

# RESOURCES

## Audio

Yo-Yo Ma has made many recordings.
This is a very select list, all of which are also available through streaming.

*Appalachian Journey*, with Edgar Meyer and Mark O'Connor, Sony Classical SK 66782, 2000, compact disc.

*The Essential Yo-Yo Ma*, Legacy, Sony Classical S2K 93927, 2005, compact disc.

*Hush*, with Bobby McFerrin, Sony Masterworks SK 48177, 1992, compact disc.

*Sing Me Home*, with the Silk Road Ensemble, Sony Masterworks 88875 18101 1, 2016, 2X LP Vinyl.

*Songs of Comfort and Hope*, with Kathryn Stott, Sound Postings LLC, 2020, compact disc.

*Yo-Yo Ma: Six Evolutions: Bach Cello Suites*, Sony Classical, 19075 85465 2, 2018, compact disc.

## Short Videos

"7-Year-Old Cellist Prodigy Yo-Yo Ma's Debut Performance for President JFK," The Kennedy Center, video, 6:09, May 29, 2020, originally filmed November 29, 1962, www.youtube.com/watch?v=wiwkBFR6rWo.

"UN Messenger of Peace Yo-Yo Ma adds his voice to TOGETHER," United Nations, June 20, 2017, video, 4:37, featuring a performance of "Song of the Birds" by Pablo Casals, www.youtube.com/watch?v=JiqVY_V7row.

"Yo-Yo Ma, cellist," interviewed by Fred McFeely Rogers, *Mister Rogers' Neighborhood*, 1985, video, 13:16, www.misterrogers.org/videos/yo-yo-ma/.

"Yo-Yo Ma: NPR Tiny Desk Concert," NPR Music, August 24, 2018, video, 12:09, featuring performances of "Prelude (from Suite No. 1 for Solo Cello)," "Sarabande (from Suite No. 6 for Solo Cello)," and "Gigue (from Suite No. 3 for Solo Cello)" by J.S. Bach, www.youtube.com/watch?v=3uiUHvET_jg.

# SELECT BIBLIOGRAPHY

## Books

Chippendale, Lisa A. *Yo-Yo Ma: A Cello Superstar Brings Music to the World*, Enslow Publishing, 2004.

Ma, Mariana. *My Son, Yo-Yo*, as told to John A. Rallo, The Chinese University of Hong Kong Press, 1996.

Ma, Yo-Yo. *Yo-Yo Ma: Beginner's Mind*, performed by Yo-Yo Ma, Audible Books, 2021, Audible audio, 1 hr., 32 mins.

## Articles and Interviews

Blum, David, "A Process Larger Than Oneself: Profile of the Cellist Yo-Yo Ma," in *Quintet: Five Journeys Toward Musical Fulfillment*, (Cornell University Press, 1998), first published as "Yo-Yo Ma's Musical Mind" in *The New Yorker*, April 23, 1989.

Interview with Yo-Yo Ma by Robert Hatch and William Hatch from their book, *The Hero Project* "Yo-Yo Ma" in *The Hero Project*, (McGraw Hill, 2006).

Marchese, David. "Yo-Yo Ma and the Meaning of Life," *New York Times*, November 20, 2020, www.nytimes.com/interactive/2020/11/23/magazine/yo-yo-ma-interview.html.

Tassel, Janet. "Yo-Yo Ma's Journeys," Harvard Magazine, March 1, 2000, www.harvardmagazine.com/2000/03/yo-yo-mas-journeys-html.

## Videos

*Classic Yo-Yo Ma*, directed by Jennifer Warner (EuroArts Entertainment, Towers Productions, 2001), Downloadable Video, 54:20. www.medici.tv/en/documentaries/classic-yo-yo-ma.
*Distant Echoes: Yo-Yo Ma & the Kalahari Bushmen*, directed by Robin Lough (Skyline Film and Television Productions, 1993) Video, 50:09. www.youtube.com/watch?v=9Qji1kRZ5uo.
*Extraordinary Minds: Yo-Yo Ma*, directed by Rob Massey, featuring Howard Gardner, Yo-Yo Ma (Ambassador Entertainment, Shout! Factory, 2011), DVD, 52 min.
*The Music of Strangers: Yo-Yo Ma & the Silk Road Ensemble*, directed by Morgan Neville (Tremolo Productions, Participant, 2016), DVD, 96 min.

## Websites

Yo-Yo Ma    yo-yoma.com
Silkroad    silkroad.org